NOTE: Designs are printed single-sided for your coloring convenience.

Check out **SwearWordColoringBook.com** for free adult coloring pages and info on all of my books!

Don't forget to sign up to the email list and receive free goodies from time to time!

Happy fucking coloring.

Cheap Ass! *wrapping paper*

Bow & ribbon included!

Also includes gift tag!

Use as wrapping paper or color and frame! It's up to you!

Don't spend extra on expensive wrapping paper!

* Cheap Ass Wrapping Paper is best used for small gifts and stocking stuffers such as jewelry, socks, and coal. For larger gifts, paste sheets together or say 'Fuck it!' and use toilet paper.

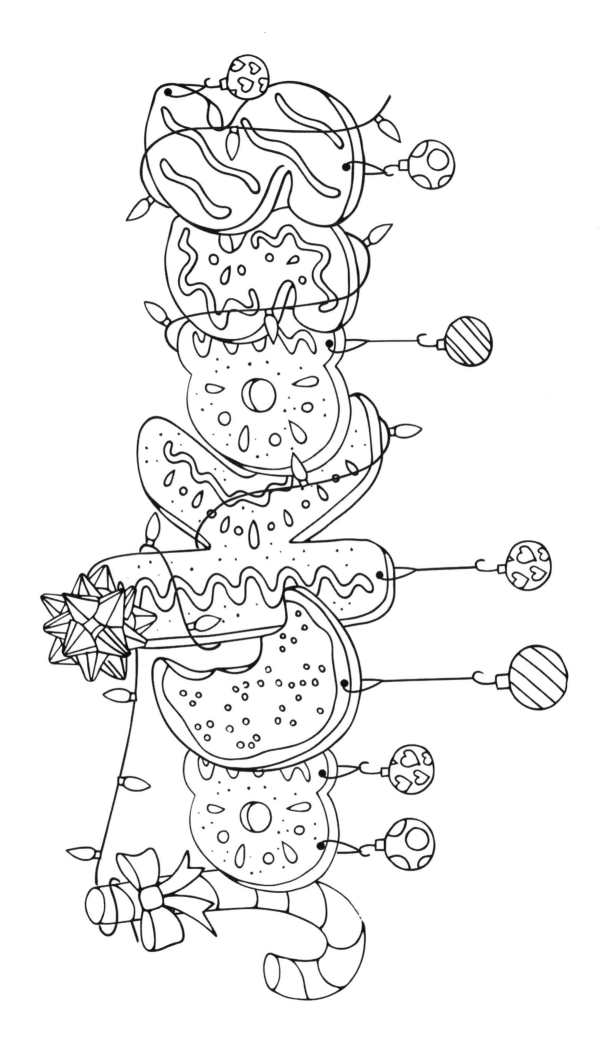

COLOR YOUR OWN FUCKING CARD.

(for a shittier result, don't use scissors, just tear!)

Shitty xmas cards

Color, cutout, fold, & give!

FUCK you.

(for a shittier result, don't use scissors, just tear!)

MERRY XMAS

you little wanker

shitty Xmas cards

FUCK you.

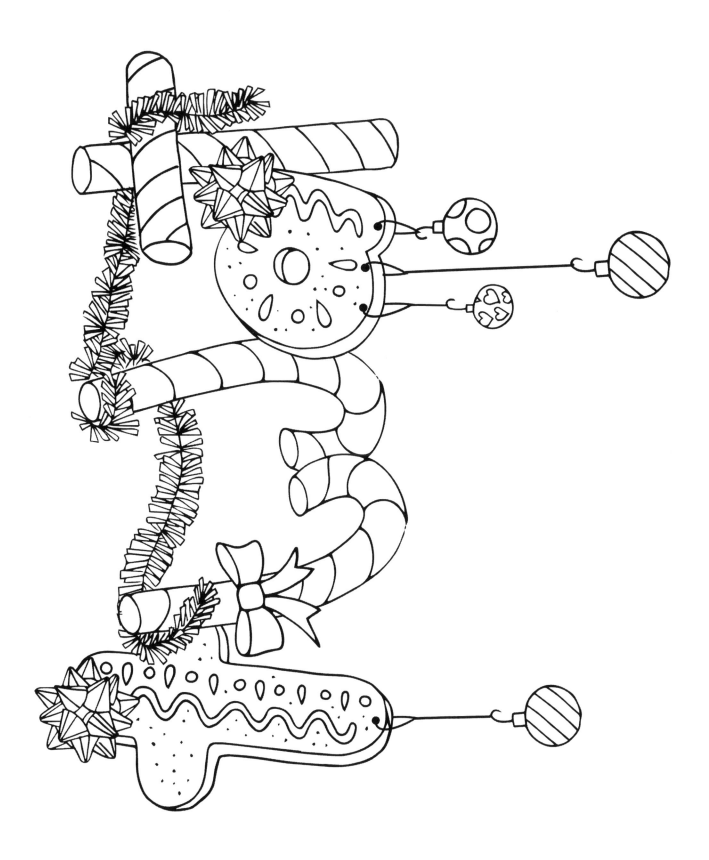

(for a shittier result, don't use scissors, just tear!)

Shitty Xmas Cards

Color, cutout, fold, & give!

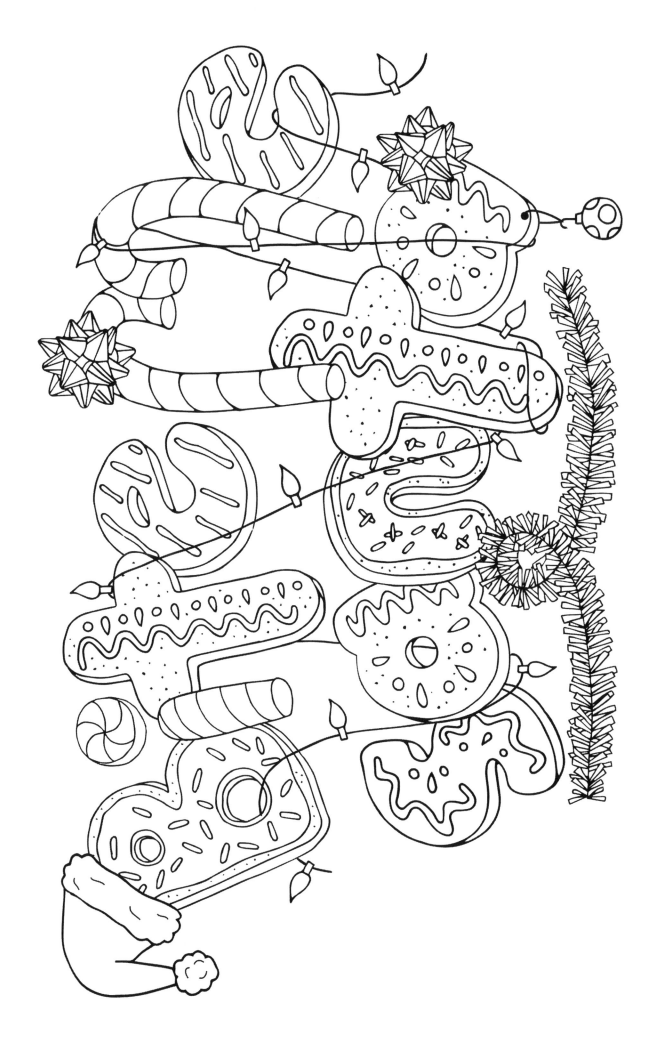

(for a shittier result, don't use scissors, just tear!)

UNWRAP THIS.

Shitty xmas cards

Color, cutout, fold, & give!

FUCK you.

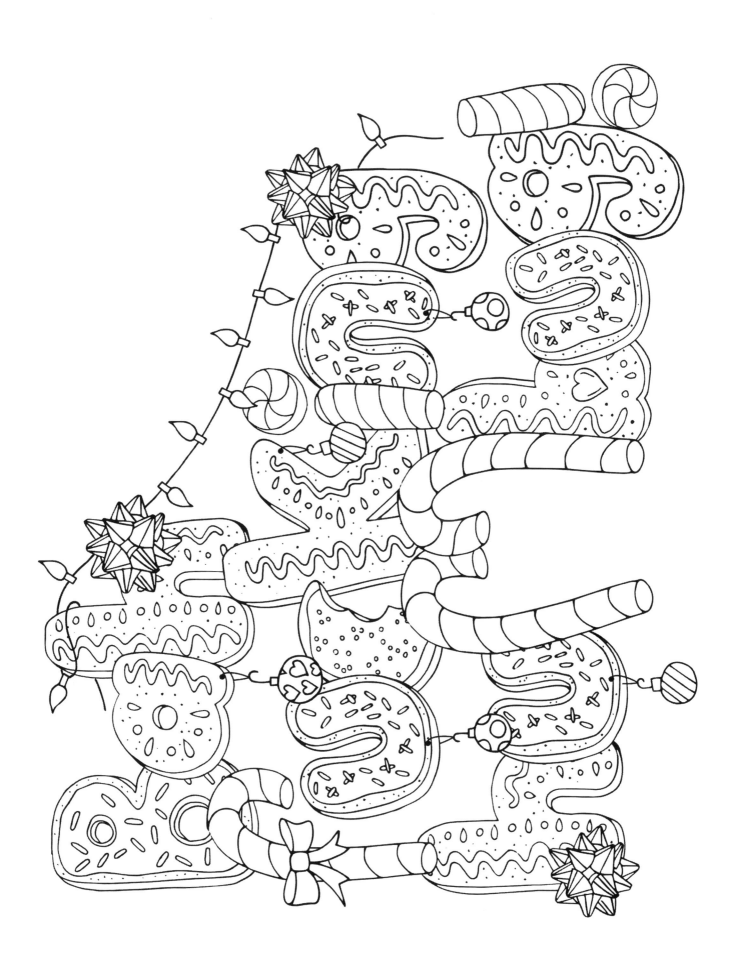

(for a shittier result, don't use scissors, just tear!)

WHERE ARE MY PRESENTS, BITCH?

Shitty Xmas Cards

Color, cutout, fold, & give!

FUCK you.

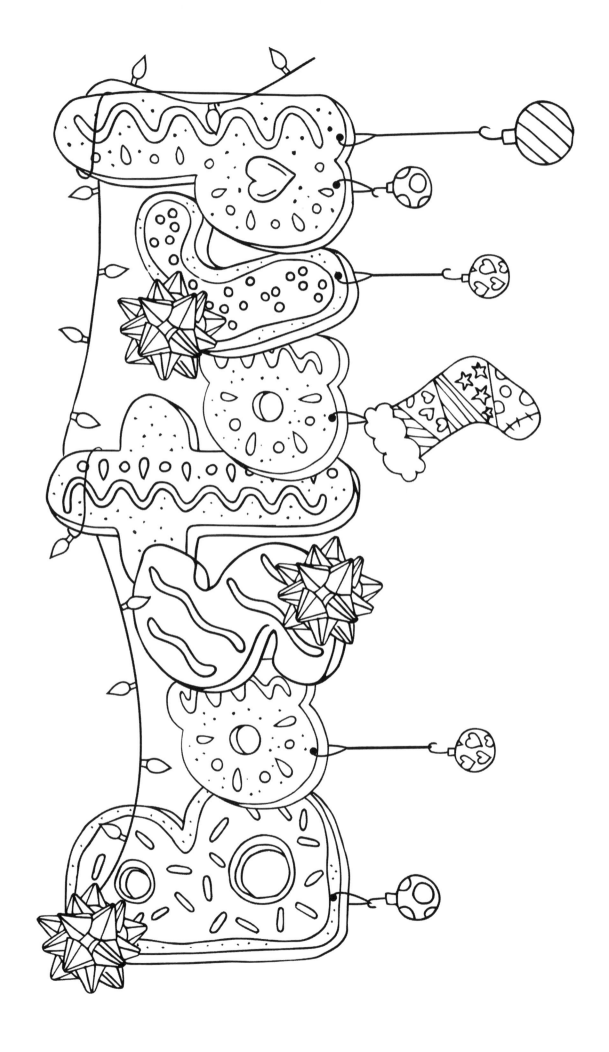

'Tis the Season

Fuck! Nothing left to color.

"The PERFECT holiday gift, just in time for New Year's Resolutions!"

The '*midnight edition*' of the best-selling motivational coloring book!

42834082R00047

Made in the USA
San Bernardino, CA
10 December 2016